History of the Baptizers Movement

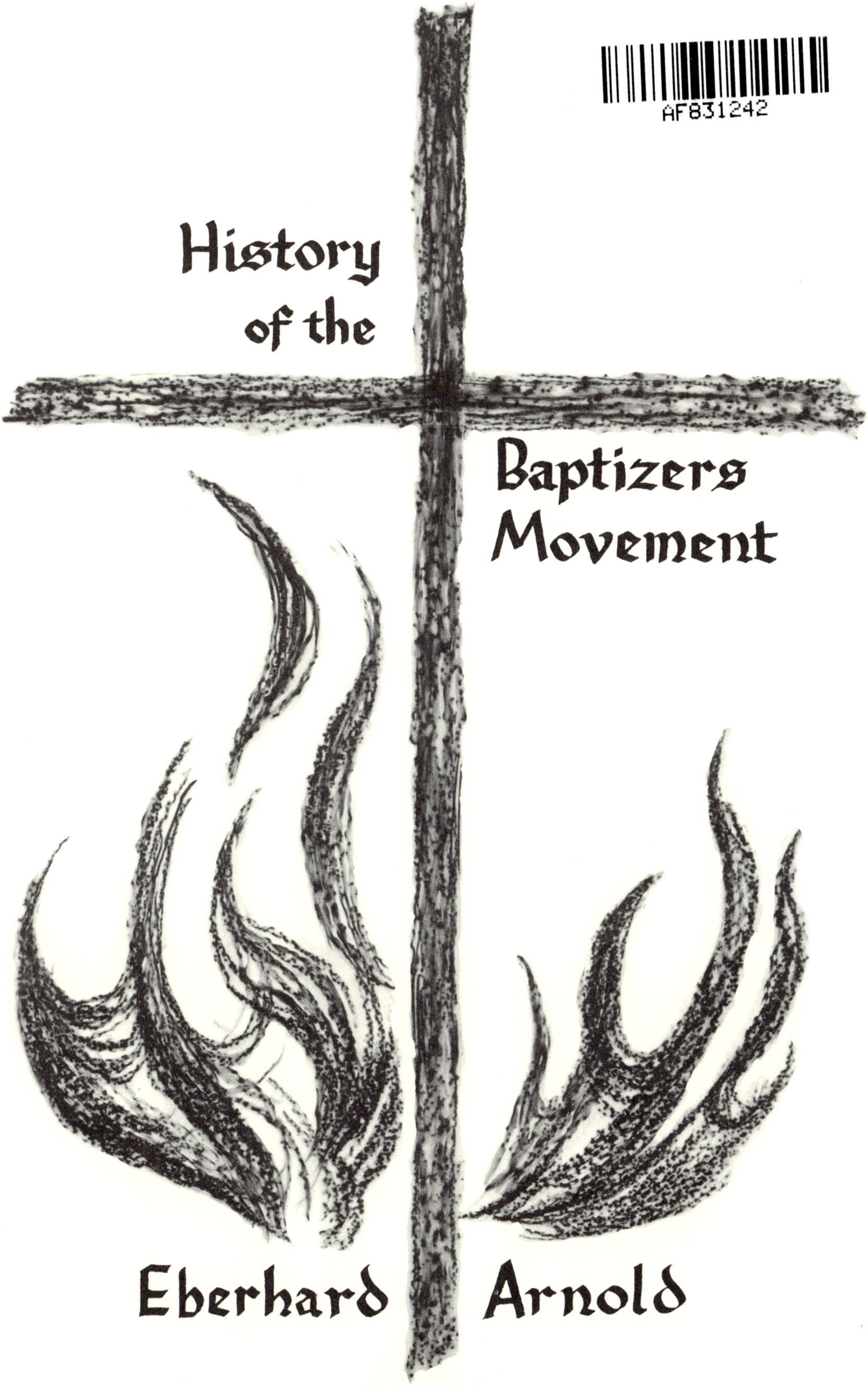

Eberhard Arnold

Edited and translated from the German
by the Society of Brothers
Rifton, New York

SBN 87486-108-X
Library of Congress Catalog Card Number: 76-98462

This article was first published in *The Mennonite Quarterly Review,* July 1969

ON THE HISTORY OF THE BAPTIZER MOVEMENT IN REFORMATION TIMES

Eberhard Arnold

Introduction

The original German manuscript is based on shorthand notes taken on November 10, 1935 (a Sunday) when Eberhard Arnold spoke to the household of the Rhön-Bruderhof (Hesse, Germany) during three successive meetings, in the morning, the afternoon, and evening. During these talks he used a copy of Ludwig Keller's *Die Reformation und die älteren Reformparteien* still preserved in the archives of the Society of Brothers in Woodcrest, Rifton, New York. Marked by Arnold, this book helped us to check and identify names, dates, titles, etc. mentioned in the lecture and enabled us to find the passages he used as a guide for these talks. However, the copy of the Keller book also shows that Arnold did not use it for the last part of the lecture and that he often quoted from memory. In most cases we were able to check and identify such references and data in the *Mennonite Encyclopedia* and in other books mentioned in the footnotes which we have provided.

Arnold was well acquainted with sixteenth-century Anabaptist writings and the books of scholars concerning this period, including the standard works by and related to Luther, Zwingli, and Calvin, as well as men like Erasmus, von Hutten, Brant, Müntzer, Schwenckfeld, Franck, and Carlstadt as far as they were available in 1935.

During his tour of the Hutterian communities in the United States and Canada in 1930-31 he tabulated all the codices and manuscripts in their possession. Until his untimely death on November 22, 1935, he was in the process of preparing a critical edition of Johannes Waldner's *Small Church Chronicle* in cooperation with Johann Loserth, the first signatures of which appeared in print. Furthermore, he was familiar with the material collected by Joseph von Beck, and studied all the important Anabaptist codices in Vienna, Gran, Brno, Pressburg, etc., and in a number of German and Dutch libraries and archives, such as Wolfenbüttel (where he discovered an old Hutterite manuscript, the "Michel-Hasel-Buch"), Herrnhut (where he found and copied much Hutterite material), the Mennonite archives in Amsterdam (where he compiled a complete list of Hutterite materials and made copies of various important documents), and others, particularly in South Germany.

When writing the footnotes to this address we tried first to verify Arnold's statements from the books he used, as far as they are still in our possession. As a further step we tried to find references for the statements made by him in the literature published after 1935. In this way we were able to verify practically all of his statements. With regard to Keller's book, we have often given page references for a longer passage in just one footnote.

4/22/74 - Plough Pub. Co. $.50 (less 20% Convention discount)

In the present translation we have tried to keep the free, spontaneous style of the original address. The use of the word "Baptizer" for *Täufer* may seem unusual, but we do not think that the words "Anabaptist" or "Baptist" convey the right meaning at all. We were happy to adopt Franklin L. Littell's term "true church" for *Gemeinde.*

In reference to Keller's theory of a continuous historical tradition leading from early Christian times to the early Anabaptists, Arnold was well aware that this theory has never been proved historically and still remains a moot question. However, apart from Keller, Sebastian Franck, in his *Chronica, Zeitbuch und Geschichtbibel,* the Hutterite *Chronicles* (*Geschichtsbücher*), the *Martyrs Mirror* (among earlier witnesses), and later authors like Füsslin (1704-73), and, more recently, Wedel, Friedmann, Williams, and others, have shown that there were at least very strong spiritual affinities between the early Anabaptists on the one hand, and the Waldenses, Paulicians, the Major Party of the Unity in Bohemia, to mention only some of the important medieval movements, on the other hand.

Finally, it should be said that the main point of Arnold's address is not to give evidence in support of a *historical* continuity, but to demonstrate that there always existed a *spiritual* continuity—i.e., that the true church never completely disappeared since apostolic times. He believed that the true church always existed somewhere, albeit driven underground and in hiding and therefore not always identifiable. "In the year 1525 the long-suppressed church began to raise her head again."

Woodcrest Archives, April, 1969

I

If we wish to grasp the significance of the movement called the Baptizing movement of the Reformation era or the Old Baptizers' movement of Reformation times, we must first realize that it was not a new movement that had never previously existed.

When I visited Bertha W. Clark[1] in Chicago, her first significant question was, "From where did this tiny flickering flame of the Baptizing movement come that appeared in so many places in Switzerland and Tirol? What was its source? Where did it come from?" This question is usually answered, "All these tiny flames came from the great fire lit by the rediscovery of the Bible in the German-speaking lands." Doubtless this is true, in the main. And yet it cannot be accurate; for the Bible, especially the Gospels, had been much published even in the fifteenth century, not only in Latin, but in German as well.

With the Bible question we come straight away upon the Waldenses[2] and all the other similar movements that go with them. It was

1 See her article "The Huterian Communities. I," *The Journal of Political Economy,* XXXII (June 1924), 357-74.

2 See article "Waldenses," *ME,* IV, 874f.

Ludwig Keller,[3] Director of Archives in Basel, who first advanced the thesis that the Baptizers had their roots in movements that form an unbroken chain with the evangelical movements going back to the very earliest time of Christianity.

This thesis may be open to challenge,[4] but one cannot disregard Keller's book of 1885 on the Reformation and the Older Reform Parties.[5] The years around 1885 opened the way to an understanding of Baptizer (Anabaptist) history. During that time Joseph von Beck (1815-87)[6] and Johann Loserth (1846-1936)[7] were drawing Baptizer history more and more into the light. This was also the time when Emil Egli,[8] a minister and licentiate of theology from Zurich, published his collection of documents concerning the history of the Zurich Reformation in the years 1519-33 (*Aktensammlung zur Geschichte der Züricher Reformation in den Jahren 1519-1533*) and his work about the Zurich Anabaptists at the time of the Reformation (*Die Züricher Wiedertäufer zur Reformationszeit*) and his booklet on the history of the St. Gall Baptizers (*Die St. Galler Täufer*). At this time, too, Carl Adolf Cornelius (1819-1903) verified the origins of the Münster movement.[9] All these writers, together with several other leading church historians, demonstrated that up to that time the Baptizer movement had been unjustly treated due to the prejudices of the official church.

For anyone who pays attention to the mystery of the ages in history, it is very significant that the *Didache*, the "Teaching of the Twelve Apostles,"[10] and a wealth of Gospel texts were also newly discovered at that time.[11] In addition, it was the era of new revivalist movements in connection with Oxford,[12] that spread over England, Germany, and North America.

---

3 See *ME*, III, 162f.

4 Robert Friedmann, "Old Evangelical Brotherhoods: Theory and Fact," *MQR*, XXXVI (1962), 349-54. Ernst Troeltsch, *The Social Teaching of the Christian Churches* (New York), II, 699 with note 445 and p. 704.

5 Ludwig Keller, *Die Reformation und die älteren Reformparteien* (Leipzig, 1885).

6 See *ME*, I, 258f.

7 See *ME*, III, 397-99.

8 See *ME*, II, 163.

9 *ME*, I, 714f. mentions Cornelius' smaller works (1851-53) on this movement as well as his principal work, *Geschichte des Münsterischen Aufruhrs*, I, II (1855, 1860) and part of his studies for the third volume—which he did not conclude—published in various periodicals.

10 See the forthcoming book by Eberhard Arnold, *The Rock and the Tower, the First Christians after the Death of the Apostles* (Rifton, N.Y., 1970).

11 E.g. the Oxyrhynchus Papyri, the Freer Logion, the Strasbourg Coptic Gospel Fragment, the Epistle of the Apostles, etc. See Arnold.

12 The revivalist movement, see book on the German Christian Student Movement by Karl Kupisch, *Studenten entdecken die Bibel, Die Geschichte der Deutschen Christlichen Studenten-Vereinigung* DCSV (Hamburg, 1964). D. L. Moody and Robert P. Smith, at a conference in Oxford in 1874, won German representatives for evangelism. Later John Mott's influence was widespread, especially among university students.

Considering all this it would appear as though God in his world government, through the interplay of hidden threads, intervenes in the spiritual world among men at very specific times and in very specific ways.

Keller well knew the objection which could be raised against him, that the connection of the Baptizers with earliest Christianity in an unbroken line of succession could not be proved. He says, "Here we are confronted with the same situation which until now has always given us a false conception of the Baptizers of Reformation times." Previous historians had always confined themselves to names and dates that were of prime signficance for the high policy of the state or the official churches. That which was moving quietly under the surface, that which influenced men's hearts and their way of life but did not change the state or the state churches was not recorded.

Consequently, we find among the historians of Jesus' day practically nothing about the existence of Jesus, the son of Mary. There are in fact only two passages, by Tacitus and Josephus, and even these are contested. Notice was taken of the movements which were based on the four Gospels only when their leaders collided with the state or the state churches. Yet they avoided this collision, since they had no desire to seek martyrdom for its own sake; they wanted to get on with their work. Certainly, they were ready at all times to be martyred if this was unavoidable—unavoidable in the sense that shirking martyrdom would have betrayed the truth.

Thus the history of the Baptizers at the time of the Reformation is met with in the documents of state and state-church authorities only insofar as clashes took place with these great powers. It follows, then, that the movement must have been much stronger than appears in these documents. The same is true of the so-called old evangelical movements and their interconnections that stretch from the first to the sixteenth centuries. Keller traces the origins of the Waldensian movement back to the "Poor of Christ," who existed long before the twelfth century. The year 1218 is important. Yet one can discern the movement commonly known as the Waldenses even as far back as 1150. For example, we know that in that year the inquisitors of Cologne reported that these "heretics" baptized adults, basing their faith on the Gospel of Mark 16:16, and that for the sake of this baptism "they went into death not only patiently, but with enthusiasm."[13]

Thus in the twelfth and thirteenth centuries we find powerful movements claiming the title "Apostolic Brothers." Keller concludes from this that these movements were connected with similar trends in the fifth and sixth centuries, since at that time decrees were issued against "heretics" that point to exactly the same kind of movement.[14] Departure from the "true rule of faith" was already in those early days—as well as later in

13 Keller, 17-19, 23 with note 3.

14 *Ibid.*, 395f.

1150–declared to be sin and heresy, a crime against the state. Some say that this movement, commonly known as the Waldensian movement but calling itself simply "Christian Brothers," goes back as far as the year AD 315, to the time of Pope Sylvester.[15]

Here we come very close to Tertullian and the Montanists.[16] In the year 1250 we learn the following from an inquisitor of the Roman church. He says, "They [the Waldenses] are the greatest danger to the church because they go back farthest, so that one can say they have existed since the time of Pope Sylvester."[17]

This same inquisitor says, secondly, "There is hardly any country in which this movement is not to be found." Thirdly, he considered the movement to be so dangerous because "they speak no blasphemies but excel with their great piety." At the same time, this inquisitor continued:

> These heretics are to be recognized by their way of life and their manner of speech. Their lives are orderly and modest, without arrogance. Their dress is neither costly nor disorderly. They speak no untruth and avoid every oath or deception. They do not seek riches. They are chaste and lead pure lives. They are moderate in eating and drinking. They never go to a tavern for dancing or other such wanton pleasures. They are industrious, teaching and learning much. They are recognized by their modest speech that completely avoids exaggeration. One never hears a useless word from them, no evil backbiting toward their fellow men. They avoid every oath.

The inquisitor comes to the conclusion that they are all the more dangerous![18]

David of Augsburg, another famous inquisitor during the thirteenth century, reports, "The 'Poor of Lyons' and the other Brothers like them are all the more dangerous, the more they are adorned in piety and appear humble and modest."[19]

Because they were persecuted so severely by the Inquisition, they had to keep as quiet as possible. Therefore there appear in the fourteenth century names such as *Winkeler* and *Grubenheimer,* signifying those who were at home in hide-outs and who were to be found in the woods. At the same time they also had the names, "the good," "the pure," "the perfect." Strangely enough, the word "heretic," in its German form, *Ketzer,* is derived from the Greek word *katharos,* meaning "pure." Further, they were called *spirituales*–men of the Spirit, and *enthusiastae.* From all these names we are able to understand the character of the movement.[20]

The name that was given to these old movements in all its varied expressions was applied to the Baptizers as well. This is true of all the names

---

15 *Ibid.,* 1f., 66.

16 See Arnold, major section "Proclamation and Prophecy."

17 Keller, 5, note 1 referring to "*Summa de Catharis et Leonistis,*" *ca.* 1250.

18 *Ibid.,* 5f.

19 *Ibid.,* 7f.

20 *Ibid.,* 9, 71.

I have mentioned here, including such odd names as *Grubenheimer* and *magistri barbati,* which means "bearded masters." This name was applied to both the Waldensian movement and the early Baptizer movement.[21]

There is a lot that could still be said about the previous history of the Brothers. There is, however, no doubt that the movement at the time of Peter Waldo (*ca.* 1177), who is quite wrongly considered to be the founder of the Waldenses, is closely connected with the movement at the time of Arnold of Brescia,[22] who died in Italy in 1155. Peter Waldo was simply a new reformer and spokesman of the movement, not its founder.[23]

The Waldenses, then, belonged to the movement that traced its origins back to the pupils and disciples and apostles of Jesus Christ. They were of the opinion that true Christianity was finally rooted out in the days of the Emperor Constantine and of Pope Sylvester in the fourth century, from AD 315 on, whereas until that time the forces of primitive Christianity had still been struggling against those of the great official church. This is a thesis that is fully confirmed by modern historical scholarship, although there is a tendency to put the date still further back, to the time of Tertullian. Pope Nicholas, too, often plays a part.

The Waldenses and related movements claimed that the authority of the apostles to bind and to loose was the basis of their faith and life. They further appealed to the apostolic commission which demanded an itinerant life in complete poverty and without any possessions, to proclaim the Gospel to men. Their attitude to the state was one of great freedom. They knew they would have to be persecuted by the state, that that was necessary; and note well that this would be done by *every* type of state. "Freedom and the Gospel" was the watchword of such men as Arnold of Brescia and Peter Waldo. By the "Gospel" they meant the words of Jesus, especially the Sermon on the Mount,[24] and the life of Jesus with his redemption. Their freedom was based on the Gospels. They desired no other freedom. Therefore their watchword was the following of Christ, the *imitatio Christi,* the imitation of Christ.

Within the Catholic church, Francis of Assisi and Thomas à Kempis belong to this movement in its broadest sense, as can be proved historically. Certainly, Francis of Assisi represented the poverty of discipleship of Christ without the freedom of the Gospel. Certainly, too, Thomas à Kempis represented discipleship without the freedom of the Gospel. In spite of this they were part of the wider circle embraced by and under the influence of this powerful movement.[25]

Around 1177 this movement penetrated deep into Germany, especially to Frankfurt, Nürnberg, and Bohemia. Already then we find the sign of

---

21 *Ibid.*, 11f.

22 See Elgin S. Moyer, *Who Was Who in Church History* (Chicago, 1968), 19f.

23 Keller, 17.

24 See Eberhard Arnold, *Salt and Light. Talks and Writings on the Sermon on the Mount* (Rifton, N.Y., 1967).

25 Keller, 18f., 21f., 66. See Friedmann, "Old Evangelical Brotherhoods," 349.

adult baptism, the strictest conception of marriage, the rejection of the great church, the readiness to accept death enthusiastically for the sake of their convictions.[26]

The Brothers had their own bishop, their own elder, among the itinerant preachers. They claimed an apostolic succession for themselves. They state that in 1215 the first epoch of apostolic succession led to a second period.[27]

This was a time when very severe persecution swept over them. In Strasbourg alone five hundred were arrested in 1212, people of all walks of life. This shows how strong the movement must have been at that time in Strasbourg (which, by the way, also throws a remarkable light on the later activity of Meister Eckhardt in Strasbourg). The prisoners testified that there were many of them in Switzerland, Italy, in Germany, and Bohemia. At that time eighty were burned at the stake. Their elder and bishop was a man named Johannes, who was among those burned. Face to face with death, he said, "We are all sinners; but not because of our faith, nor because of the vices of which we are accused without cause. We expect forgiveness of our sin from God, but without human help and without the mediation of priests."[28]

It must be added that the "Poor of Christ" (by which name the Franciscans were also known, who were called *minores* or lesser ones, proletarians) prove that there existed a link between the Waldenses and the Beguines and Beghards. These latter were active long before 1370. They were similar to the third order of St. Francis. The Beguines were the women, the Beghards the men.

The Beguines as sisters and the Beghards as brothers kept communal households, lived in community of goods. They concerned themselves in particular with the poor and the weak, with folk who were physically or mentally handicapped. For themselves they also chose poverty and a life without possessions. The utmost simplicity in dress was required, without conforming to fashion. Therefore their dress developed a certain uniformity, though it did not really become like a monastic garb. They cared for the homeless, the poor, the weak, and the sick, and thus became the forerunners of the deaconesses. They concerned themselves with education and were the forerunners of rural boarding schools. They had communities of work. We read of such congregations as early as 1230 where the Poor lived together and worked for the poor. Their opponents spoke ironically of their places as "poorhouses" and "workhouses"— ridicule that could apply to the present-day bruderhofs as well. They themselves, however, called their communal settlements "Houses of God."

They tackled the social problem in a particularly earnest way, as well as the religious one. They solved it by having their goods in common

---

26 Keller, 23 with note 3.

27 *Ibid.*, 25, note 6, 71.

28 *Ibid.*, 26; Thieleman J. van Braght, *Martyrs Mirror* (Scottdale, 1951), 309f.

and by working in community. And while tackling the religious-social problem they came to grips with the educational problem as well and solved it through the establishment of special educational centers and schools. As a result people gave them the nickname, "the young folks' good people." They were also called "the good boys." They called themselves "apostles," however, a name that was current not just since the time of Peter Waldo, who was active in southern France around 1176, but much earlier. The Archbishop Henry of Cologne said in 1306 that these people had been called "Beguines, Beghards and apostles" since old times! They were also called "Friends of God," especially in the Rhine district; also "Apostolic Brothers," "bearded men," and "witnesses." The movement with which we are concerned was a large one indeed.[29]

What these movements represented was the following. They confessed to the inspiration of Christ's Spirit. They confessed that the Bible and especially the Gospels were inspired, and also their apostles. They confessed particularly to the words of Jesus, to his commands and his commissions. They believed that he was with them according to his promise, "Lo, I am with you always, unto the end of the world." They believed that the Holy Spirit as the Spirit of truth entered into the hearts of those who were dedicated to Christ. Thus they believed that the same Spirit was at work in the Gospels and in the words of the apostles. They attached special importance to the words of Christ, considering them "evangelical commandments"; the Roman Catholic Church calls the same words "the evangelical counsel."[30]

Christ's whole life was an example to them. They wished to follow him and to go the same way that he had gone. Therefore they followed the "evangelical commandment" or "evangelical counsel" that they should deny themselves and follow Jesus. Thus they liked to call themselves "followers of Christ." Their lives were to be no different from the life of Jesus as he himself had lived it, in both its inner nature and outer expression.

Their inner stand was faith in the Spirit of truth. They believed that this Spirit is imparted to all his disciples. He brings healing and strengthening of the will, consisting in freedom of will. The Spirit makes the inward eye sharp to differentiate good from evil, the Christ-like from the antichrist-like. The Spirit of truth illumines the heart through deepest inner revelation. He writes the Word of God into heart and conscience. Jesus' redemption and the discipleship of Christ become reality in the heart through Christ's Spirit.

For the apostolic Brothers the inner light is the seed, the grain of salt of Christ's power. The inner light constantly reminds us of all that Jesus said, and especially of his Sermon on the Mount. For these Brothers

29 Keller, 28-35. See also *ME*, I, 264f.

30 For the above and the following six paragraphs on the confession of these movements see Keller, 36-62, 354-56.

the Sermon on the Mount is the *evangelion katexochen*—the Gospel at its sharpest and most definite, and in its clearest, most comprehensive form. As a result, the Brothers always stressed these words, "Deal with others as you would have them deal with you."

Mercy and purity are the characteristics of this new attitude toward men. If I want to do to men what I hope they will do for me, I cannot be richer than my fellow men. I may neither judge them nor criticize them hatefully. Nor can I kill them, whatever spirit may order this killing.[31] I cannot, for my part, recognize or carry out any death sentence. Therefore I cannot hold any public office, because I live only for the Kingdom of peace and love, as Jesus lived for it. I cannot serve any vengeance, either personal or national. Even self-defense is denied to me as a follower of Jesus. Discipleship of Jesus binds me to such honesty and trust that I can neither accept nor take any oath. I am called to such great trust that I must love my enemies with an especial trust.

In this context one of the Waldenses said, "Love to one's friends alone is a small love. The great and all-embracing love is such as loves even its enemies." Therefore we cannot answer abuse with abuse or avenge evil with evil.

All this was represented by the Brothers due to the working of the true church among them; for the direct, spontaneous working of grace is bound up with the true church. Whoever follows Christ and obeys his words belongs to his church. True love is possible only where God is loved; this is to love the church and to love one's enemies. So much for the antecedents of this movement (the Anabaptist movement).

II

The original Baptizer movement was closely connected with these earlier movements. We see this in the fact that in Basel and Zurich the Brothers who later founded the Baptizer movement took part in the meetings of these movements, according to existing records. By their opponents this "circle of spirituals" was called a "school of heretics." The founders of the Baptizers moved in both circles, in Basel as well as in Zurich.[32]

The basic ideas, which can be found as early as 1515 in Basel and Zurich, are the same which the Baptizers represented later. Staupitz, too, represented the same principles in Nürnberg as early as 1515. Basel was a center of the German book trade and printing. Nürnberg was a center for all the brotherly movements, all the spiritual and artistic concerns of that time. Luther was led to the Gospel by Staupitz. Staupitz had contact with the "old evangelical church" through the old patrician

31 Karl Kautsky in his book *Vorläufer des neueren Sozialismus,* Vol. II: *Der Kommunismus in der deutschen Reformation* (Stuttgart, 1913), 128-29, also stresses the peace-loving tendencies of the Waldenses and the Beghards in Switzerland.

32 Keller, 336, 395-99; Kautsky, 137-39. See also J. Warns, *Die Taufe* (Bad Homburg, 1913), 94.

families in Nürnberg. This can be shown especially in the case of the Tucher family, but it also comes out with Albrecht Dürer[33] and Hans Sachs. Grebel and Manz were Zwingli's friends. Manz had been at home in the circles of the "Old Brothers" in Basel and Zurich.[34]

It is clear, then, that in the movement known as the Baptizer movement we are not dealing with a human invention or the ideas of individuals. The "school of heretics" in Zurich and also in St. Gall was called "reading of the spirituals," because they read old heretical writings and especially the Bible.[35]

It can be proved that Zwingli was in contact with the "school of heretics" in Zurich. Zwingli's original opposition to charging interest, to capitalism, stems from this "school of heretics." As late as 1523 Grebel wrote to his brother-in-law, Joachim Vadian,[36] who was a member of the Great Council of St. Gall, that interest and tithes would soon be abolished in Zurich with Zwingli's agreement. Unfortunately, he had to write a month later that Zwingli had defected from his own convictions and had agreed with the decision of the Council, which had come out in favor of tithes and of charging interest. This came about because Zwingli was convinced that the emerging reformed church could not exist without the help of the state.[37]

The attitude toward the state is the decisive difference between Zwingli and those who until then had been his friends. But note well—the attitude to the state resulting from the attitude to the true church! Zwingli was of the opinion that the state's cultural task must be supported; in the hands of the state, the organized church must serve the state's cultural task; and the state must be Christianized.[38]

The separation between Zwingli and Grebel, who had been particularly close friends, had to do with the concept of the church and the concept of the state, the problem of church and state. The two go together; not the church problem apart from the state problem, but the two seen together as one problem—this is what divided Zwingli and Grebel. This was at all times clear to Zwingli, and he expressed it repeatedly. He said, for instance, "Baptism in itself would not be important enough for us to arrest and execute people." Zwingli himself often declared infant baptism to be unjustified. "But," he continued, "we had to resist the Baptizers because we noticed that in baptism they had found the symbol that represented their dissenting attitude towards church

---

33 See *Mennonitisches Lexikon* (Frankfurt, 1913), I, 486-93.

34 Keller, 323-27, 333, 339f.

35 See Leonhard von Muralt, *Glaube und Lehre der Schweizerischen Wiedertäufer in der Reformationszeit* (Zurich, 1938), 8f.; also Emil Egli, *Die St. Galler Täufer* (Zurich, 1887), 12f.; Harold S. Bender, *Conrad Grebel c. 1498-1526* (Goshen, 1950), 90; George H. Williams, *The Radical Reformation* (Philadelphia, 1962), 128.

36 See *ME*, IV, 796.

37 Keller, 400-403; Kautsky, 139f; Ernest Müller, *Geschichte der Bernischen Täufer* (Frauenfeld, 1895), 8.

38 Muralt, 14-16; Müller, 8.

and state." Zwingli constantly referred to things said by Grebel and others: "There is no better way of coming to grips with the state or of eluding it than through baptism." In this very concern for the true church in opposition to Roman Catholicism and in the concern about injustice in opposition to the state, baptism was the symbol for the Baptizers of the separation of church and state.[39]

Waldensian tradition already had always declared that apostles of Jesus Christ cannot fulfil any political function. The believing church of Jesus Christ cannot uphold any political state order. The believing church follows Jesus Christ's commands and thus needs no state laws. The state exists for the suppression of evil in an ungodly and satanic world. It is not for the believing disciples of Jesus Christ to suppress evil in the outer world; they are redeemed from evil.[40]

Zwingli conceived of the church as a state-constituted society based on law. The church of the Brothers was a community of heart and life based on the Spirit. It could be a voluntary church only; it could be a church only through the inspiration of the Spirit.[41] Thus as early as October 1523 Simon Stumpf said to Zwingli that he should on no account give the power of abolishing the mass to the Zurich City Council—that is, to the government. As a Christian, he said, Zwingli had no authority to place such religious matters as the abolition of the mass in the hands of the government.[42]

Two years before the abolition of the mass, Stumpf said, "Master Ulrich, you do not have the right to place the decision on this matter in the hands of my lords, for the decision has already been made, the Spirit of God decides."[43] The believing representatives of the later Baptizer movement said, two years before they advocated baptism, that state authorities cannot be allowed to have anything to do with the church, and vice versa. Luther and Zwingli achieved tremendous success outwardly by going along with the power of the state; for the ideas of reformation they represented had long been advocated in the clearest possible way by the brotherly movements, perhaps for centuries before their time, but then especially by Staupitz and the other Brothers. By resorting to the power of the state Luther and Zwingli betrayed the Gospel because they wanted to win the masses. They represented the idea that the Gospel is too high for the common people to live up to![44]

---

39 Kautsky, 154-56; Richard Nitsche, *Geschichte der Wiedertäufer in der Schweiz zur Reformationszeit* (Einsiedeln and New York, 1885), 40; J. Loserth, *Georg Blaurock und die Anfänge des Anabaptismus in Graubündten und Tirol* (Berlin, 1899), 16; Bender, 99f., 157-59; Williams, 96f.

40 Keller, 91f.

41 Muralt, 44-47; Cornelius Bergmann, *Die Täuferbewegung im Kanton Zürich bis 1660* (Leipzig, 1916), 18.

42 Keller, 405f.; Müller, 8f.

43 Bender, 98.

44 See *ME*, II, 574; *ME*, III, 421f.; Müller, 6f.; Walther Köhler, *Das Buch der Reformation Huldrych Zwinglis* (München, 1931), 182-84.

The distinguishing characteristics, then, can be clearly recognized. For example, Zwingli could on no account accept the refusal to take an oath. He himself said, "To the *Eidgenossen* [the "Comrades of the Oath," as the Swiss called themselves], the oath has since old times been a solemn declaration of their allegiance to the state. It is therefore an unavoidable necessity."[45] To the Brothers this title *Schweizer Eidgenossen* was repugnant, because it proved the whole antichristian nature of the Swiss state.

The same contrast was to be seen in the question of the bearing of arms, the question of nonviolence. For Zwingli the bearing of arms was the crown of his republican consciousness, the citizen's badge of honor, a sign of love for the fatherland.[46] And so he fell in the battle of Kappel in 1531. Zwingli wanted the state to control matters of faith. The apostolic Brothers declared that the state had nothing to do with these matters. The state cannot exist without law court, sword, and prison. To the Brothers, every kind of mixing of the things of the state with the apostolic task was an insult to the apostles.

So the Brothers, including the later Baptizers, demonstrated again and again that the state existed on the basis of Roman law, that the republican as well as the imperial states lived according to the imperial law of the Romans, and that therefore the nature of the state was pagan and Roman, not even Old-Testament and Mosaic.[47] For them it had nothing to do with the Gospel of Jesus and with his Sermon on the Mount. The separation of Zwingli from his friends thus had to be an extreme one. The antithesis had to reach its ultimate climax. Unfortunately this went so far that Zwingli agreed to the execution of his former friend Felix Manz.[48]

For a time Nürnberg and Basel became the two centers that replaced Strasbourg, the former center of the brotherly movement. We will not deal so much with Nürnberg at this point, because that historical line leads particularly to Luther, Müntzer, Staupitz, and Hans Hut. Between Nürnberg and Basel there was a very close contact, especially of the Nürnberg printers and artists with those of Basel. The outstanding printers in Basel were Amerbach, Froben, and Petri. Eminent artists, scholars, and able business men were active in the print shops, such as Pamphilus Gengenbach, Andreas Cratander, and Valentin Curio. These names point to a strong tie with Zwingli and the Brothers in Zurich, for Basel had a strong influence upon Zurich, while on the other hand Basel also had very strong connections with Lyons and other Waldensian centers, for example with Franz Lambert of Avignon. Hans Holbein, too, kept up a lively

---

45 Muralt, 45; Müller, 12.

46 Müller, 12.

47 *Ibid.*, 13.

48 Zwingli even made the terrible statement, "You must baptize an Anabaptist again and again until he is drowned." See G. Bonnet-Maury, *Early Sources of English Unitarian Christianity*, tr. by Edward P. Hall (London, 1884), 43.

contact with these circles and supplied wood cuts for various books printed in Basel.[49]

In no other century have men of science, art, and craftsmanship worked together in so brotherly a way as was the case here in Basel. Hans Holbein and Hans Frank in particular were part of the "Brotherhood of Heaven." This brotherhood in Basel accepted into membership especially lovers of craftsmanship, printers, and scholars. At that time Erasmus of Rotterdam also lived in Basel and kept in touch with this circle. Oecolampadius, the reformer of Basel, and Hans Denck had contact with Erasmus' inner circle as early as 1515. To this circle there also belonged a close friend of the young patrician Conrad Grebel; this friend was Heinrich Loriti from Ennenda in Glarus, called Glareanus, who had dealings with other people in Basel as well. Apart from him, those especially worthy of mention are Michael Bentinus, a friend of Hans Denck, Richard Crocus, Wolfgang Capito, and Johann Oecolampadius.[50]

The interest of this circle, which met in chapter brotherhoods, was concentrated on the New Testament, the study of Greek language and grammar, and such scholarly research as was important to them for the better understanding of the New Testament. In 1523 Hans Denck edited a large complete edition of the grammar of Theodore Gaza of Thessalonica in the Greek language, which was printed by Valentin Curio. On the title page Denck wrote a verse in Greek, revealing his identity as the editor:

Anagnōstē Degkios
Aonos hostis erās glukerēn kepoio tithēnēn
Tauta soi euodmon biblia thēke rhodon.
(For any reader who loves the gentle gardener of a riverbank garden,
Denck plants this book as a fragrant rose.)[51]

From Basel, Erasmus wrote in 1516:

> I am in a veritable seat of the Muses. There is no one here in Basel who does not know Latin and Greek, and most of them Hebrew too. One person is better versed in history, another in mathematics, or antiquities, or jurisprudence.

He was particularly impressed by the mutual friendship and harmony prevalent in this circle.[52]

Oecolampadius wrote to Pirkheimer at Nürnberg that one of the main principles of the community founded later had already been expounded in this circle in 1515. As early as 1514 the Roman Catholic sacrament of the altar was being attacked at Basel. Thus Oecolampadius shows that the ideas of the Baptizers, as they were called, were being expressed in Switzerland as early as 1515. The Director of Archives, Keller, adds,

---

49 Keller, 327f.; Kautsky, 35.
50 Keller, 328-30; Kautsky, 130, 132.
51 Keller, 330f.
52 *Ibid.*, 332.

"Not as though something new had been discovered, but because these were the old ideas of the brotherhood."[53]

We have no time to go into the old Bible translations, as there are many incunabula of the Bible in German traceable to the period before the year 1500; and in the fifteenth century ninety-eight complete editions of the Bible in Latin were in circulation. In Germany eighteen complete Bible editions and many part editions appeared in German between 1466 and 1518. As early as 1494 Sebastian Brant's poem *Narrenschiff* ("Ship of Fools") said quite rightly, "All lands are now full of the Holy Scriptures." It is very striking that in these old Bibles the likeness of the pope was painted among the devils of apocalyptic hell. This shows that these Bibles were not published by the Catholics but by the Brothers' circles which later merged with the Baptizer circles.[54]

Only at this point can we appreciate the significance of the words found in the Hutterian histories about the year 1525, "In the year 1525 the long-suppressed church [or church-community] began to raise her head again."[55] That is to say, this true church, this community, had previously been there, but now she raised her head as she had not done before. She raised her head in the sense that she no longer worked in obscurity but in the broadest spheres of public life. The first great period of the Baptizer movement brought such great numbers of people under its spell and had such an impetus of Spirit and power that it was equal in influence and importance to the Catholic and Protestant churches of that time.[56]

The true name of the supporters of this movement was not "Baptizers," still less "Anabaptists" (which means Re-baptizers); but it was simply "Christians" and "Brothers." Their name was simply "Evangelicals," which is what they had called themselves for many centuries. Consequently the writings of the Brothers in Zurich since 1525 speak of the Zwinglians and Lutherans as "New Evangelicals" and of themselves as "Evangelicals," as those who conform to the Gospels. Later, when they were being suppressed by the state, they called themselves "Old Evangelicals" in contrast to the Lutherans and the "New Evangelicals," because their name was derived exclusively from the Gospel, and their deeds as well were in accordance with the Gospel.[57]

Love is the hallmark of their faith. It is the sum total of their being.

53 *Ibid.*, 332f.

54 *Ibid.*, 280, 334, 335 with note 1, 336, 394f.; Bergmann, 12f.; Ludwig von Gerdtell, *Brennende Fragen der Weltanschauung . . .*, Vol. IV: *Die Revolutionierung der Kirchen* (Schöneiche bei Berlin-Friedrichshagen, 1921), 162f., note 1. Robert Friedmann, "A Hutterite Book of Medieval Origin," *MQR*, XXX (1956), 65-71.

55 Josef Beck, *Die Geschichts-Bücher der Wiedertäufer in Oesterreich-Ungarn* (Wien, 1883), 12, note 1, from Codex O in Gran, 1525-1581.

56 Keller, 364-66; Williams 846.

57 Keller, 11, 367 with note 3. See also article "Anabaptist" by H. S. Bender in *ME*, I, 113f.

This one can see in all their songs and confessions, and in the records of their martyrdom.

This movement, then, was a renewal of the old brotherly movement, which emerged quietly between the years 1515 and 1523. In the time from 1523 to 1525 it broke forth into the public eye in Zurich. Grebel's religious convictions, which he later confirmed by baptism, can be documented already for the year 1523. It was the time during which Conrad Grebel was staying in Zurich and still was a close friend of Zwingli.[58] In the communities of the Brothers it was a matter of an inner rebirth and of a powerful emergence of an older movement. This inner rebirth of the true church, of the brotherhood and of apostolic itinerant mission, had first been prepared in scholarly thinking during the period 1515-1523 in Basel and Zurich.[59]

Basel was the foremost meeting place of the men who were later to lead the movement. Hubmaier, Denck, and Grebel are the well-known names of those who were in Basel at that time. It is interesting to read what Jean Canaye, a Frenchman, wrote in 1524, that Basel at that time had become a haven of refuge and salvation for them: "Basel is truly a royal city, for the King of kings wants his Gospel and his eternal laws to flourish and to be read and proclaimed there!"[60]

Until 1525 the advocates of the evangelical movement in Basel championed the same point of view concerning the Gospels which Grebel later defended in Zurich, Hubmaier in Waldshut, Denck in Nürnberg, and Oecolampadius, the reformer, in Basel itself. The struggle about baptism really began in Basel, particularly since 1523, but partly already before then. In the summer of 1524 Erasmus was aware that there were many in Basel who were opposed to infant baptism. As early as 1522 Coccinius Doggius at Basel edited certain theses by Ulrich Hugwald which he said the latter had represented already in the winter of 1521-22, among which there were six theses in favor of baptism based on confession of faith.[61]

In that same year the statutes of the "Heavenly Brotherhood," as it was called, were newly endorsed. These statutes already contain the basis for the teaching and constitution of the later Brothers known as the Baptizers. Still in 1524 there were some important chapter meetings held in Basel, as they are known to have been held by the Brothers since much earlier times. There is a document still in existence, a handwritten invitation by Hubmaier dated June 11, 1524. He invites the Brothers to come to his house with their Bibles for the next chapter meeting and mentions eighteen theses on religious questions as the agenda. He writes that for this meeting he wants to remind them of the bond of brotherly love, of the holiness of Christian peace, and of the name of the Lord

58 Bender, 96.

56 Keller, 364-66; Williams 846.

60 *Ibid.*, 373; Kautsky, 131.

61 For this and the following five paragraphs see Keller, 374-87, 388 with notes 2 and 4.

Jesus Christ. He goes on to say that these chapters or brotherhood meetings are an old custom, passed on from apostolic times; and that long ago they were, however, called synods.

The members taking part in these chapter meetings were well known in the Basel printing houses as well. The books of the old "Friends of God" were published by these houses, and also (about 1523) the writings of John Wycliffe, Johann Wessel of Groningen, and especially of Marsilius of Padua, all books by men who were excommunicated by the Roman Catholic Church as heretics. In 1522 the *Fridschirmbuch* ("Defender of Peace Book") was also printed in Basel by Valentin Curio, whose associate and corrector at that time was Hans Denck.

In 1521 Grebel appeared in these printing houses. He lived in Basel and also worked in the printing shops. He arrived there in August 1521, and his closest friends were the members of the chapter brotherhood of Denck and Hubmaier. Grebel was still a student at that time. In 1521 Dr. Ursinus calls him a "distinguished young man." Everyone praised his talents and his outstanding erudition. Vadian, the physician who later condemned him, said that he was a man of great gifts. In this period Grebel experienced his spiritual conversion and also married.

In the circle in which Grebel moved was Wilhelm Reublin[62] who was later for a short time a Hutterite brother; also a number of prominent theologians, among whom Simon Stumpf,[63] who later went to Zurich, interests us most in this context. It is very interesting that one of the later Baptizer leaders from the Grisons also came to Basel as early as 1520. This was the famous bookseller and printer Andreas Castelberger, called "Andreas on Crutches."[64] We meet him later in Zurich, St. Gall and Chur as well as in Basel. He was a close friend of Blaurock, later became a servant of the word, an apostolic messenger, and was called "limping Andreas."

So there was a constant coming and going of the apostolic Brothers in the printers' houses of Basel. Yet it was not in Basel that the movement was to experience its tremendous public outburst, but in Zurich. Basel's ties with the old-evangelical, apostolic Brothers were strong. Utmost secrecy concerning the Brothers sent out as apostles prevailed, lest they should be betrayed to the authorities and the executioners. However, we can read in a letter from Basel dated December 17, 1524, "They are called apostles, evangelists, and bishops." These are the same expressions that were used also in the circle of Grebel, Denck, and Hubmaier. This important message was written by a Petrus Tossanus.[65] Keller con-

62 See *ME,* IV, 304-07.

63 *Ibid.,* IV, 648.

64 *Ibid.,* I, 523f.; Kautsky, 131.

65 Keller, 387.

cludes from it that these apostolic messengers took part in the meetings of the "Heavenly Brotherhood."

Baptism itself, however, was not introduced until January 1525 in Zurich.[66] Zwingli considered Grebel as the leader of the movement. He was the son of Jakob Grebel, a respected Zurich patrician and councillor. Born in Zurich around 1490, he passed most of his childhood in Grüningen. He was the eldest son of seven children. His father saw to it that all seven children received a very thorough scholarly education. This was an enormous achievement for a family with seven children, even for a patrician. He sent Conrad to Vienna, Basel, Paris, and wherever he wished to go. Conrad first devoted himself to the study of the various languages and branches of learning. He went to Vienna in 1515 and stayed there until 1518. In 1518 he went to Paris to study, not theology but Latin, Greek, and Hebrew. He returned to Zurich in 1520 and there followed his bent for learning. In 1521-22 we find him in Basel, where he worked at his studies with Erasmus and was active in printing with Cratander. Now the great inner change in him took place, in 1521 and 1522. This great change was wrought in him by the influence of the circle at Basel and by Zwingli.

Now Grebel threw himself with his whole energy and the whole strength of his spiritual interest into the study of the New Testament and the entire Bible. In August 1520 Zwingli still spoke of him as an especially noble and erudite young man. But Grebel was seeking to make Jesus' demands, his life, and his discipleship the substance of his own life, in complete consistency. Thus in 1522 a sharp tension arose between Zwingli and Grebel.[67]

In Zurich, Grebel had made friends with Klaus Hottinger and Heinrich Aberli. On July 7, 1522, these three were seriously warned to discontinue speaking against the monks and to refrain altogether from discussing such matters regarding the church.[68] In 1523 Grebel and his friends undertook a very sharp attack on capital, the payment of interest and church taxes, and demanded their complete abolition. In June 1523 Grebel wrote that Zwingli was holding the same convictions and would be joining him, and that interest would be abolished. A month later he had to write, "The people of this world, our men of Zurich [i.e., the City Council] act like tyrants and Turks in the matter of tithes."[69] All of Zwingli's friends reproached him, saying that so far he had preached against the giving of tithes, but having made friends with the Council he revoked everything he said against tithes.

66 Bender, 137. For this and the following paragraphs see also article on Grebel in *ME*, II, 566-75.

67 Williams, 94f.

68 See articles on Hottinger, *ME*, II, 820f. and on Aberli, *ME*, I, 7f. Bender, 84.

69 Grebel's letters to Vadian, June 17 and July 15, 1523, in L. von Muralt and W. Schmid, *Quellen zur Geschichte der Täufer in der Schweiz, I: Zürich* (Zurich, 1952), Nos. 1, 2, pp. 1-2. See also Bender, 86, 91, 94, 106.

At the same time, however, Grebel and his friends thrust energetically forward in their quest for the true church. The true church was to consist of a Christian people living in all innocence, clinging to the Gospel and having nothing to do with interest or other forms of profiteering. So in the summer of 1523 there occurred an abrupt break with Zwingli. Stumpf and Grebel went to see Zwingli in the summer of 1523 and said to him, "You are too slow and too lukewarm in all things concerning the true church and the Kingdom of God. Don't you realize which way the times are driving? Don't you see where the Spirit of God is driving? Now is the time to act, in the greatest and holiest sincerity!"[70]

They begged Zwingli to consider that it is impossible to lead an entire city to a general uniting of Christians. He should look at the apostolic church in Jerusalem and consider how it was founded. The true church in Zurich must come into being in just the same way. The true church can be formed only by those who are gripped by the Spirit of God, only by those who are ruled and guided by the Spirit of God. Whoever follows Christ will be ready for such a life of church-community.

Above all, Stumpf and Grebel reproached Zwingli for placing decisions concerning faith and the true church in the hands of the government.[71] God's word is free! It is not for the government to rule with force over the Word of God, or even to control the preaching of God's Word by force. But Zwingli rejected these thoughts. He said he could not possibly found a church that would be independent of the state.

So the Brothers left Zwingli and founded chapter brotherhoods in the Bible-studying circles. Now the name Felix Manz crops up again, for these meetings took place at the house of Manz's mother. Felix Manz translated the Old Testament from the original Hebrew text; Grebel translated the New Testament from the Greek. They prayed to Christ that they might show a stronger faith. Soon they undertook a new attack on Zwingli, this time especially against the vestments and the ritual of the mass.[72]

Out of the religious discussions concerning these points resulted the final break between Zwingli and Grebel, in October 1523. Again the state and government were the issues. Grebel demanded a decision to abolish the mass. Zwingli declared this could be done only by the power of the state. Stumpf declared, "Zwingli, you have no right to turn these questions over to the Council. The Spirit of God has already decided them." Grebel contested Zwingli's opinion just as energetically and got into a violent argument with him. The Council was very much encouraged by Zwingli's attitude and immediately decreed that only the Word of God should be preached; that there should be no more dealings in such ques-

---

70 Muralt, 12-15; Emil Egli, *Die Züricher Wiedertäufer zur Reformationszeit* (Zurich, 1878), 13f.; Samuel Geiser, *Die Taufgesinnten-Gemeinden* (Karlsruhe, 1931), 130-32.

71 See notes 42 and 43 above.

72 Muralt, 27. See also article on Manz in *ME*, III, 472-74.

tions as interest, the mass, and so on. Everything was to stay as it was.

In November of 1523 Zwingli made a sharp attack on the Brothers who had so recently been his friends, in his *Kurze Christliche Einleitung* ("Short Christian Introduction").[73] On November 4, 1523, a friend of Grebel was exiled because he had destroyed a crucifix. His name was Hochrütiner,[74] and he returned to St. Gall. For a time Zwingli had been inclined toward the Brothers in the question of baptism as well as that of interest on money borrowed. In 1524 the struggle about infant baptism began anew in Zurich. Grebel and his friends declared infant baptism to be an abomination and a work of the devil. On September 3, 1524, Grebel wrote that he would make contact with Andreas Carlstadt and Thomas Müntzer. Perhaps he would also make a sharp attack on Martin Luther, urged by his trust in the Word of God. He reported that he was now reading the Gospel of Matthew with several listeners.[75] On September 5, 1524, the Brothers wrote an important letter to Müntzer, warning him and begging him to give up everything bordering on armed insurrection.[76] After this the contact with Müntzer was broken. On the other hand, the contact with the mystic, Carlstadt, was deeper and of longer duration. The Brothers had been corresponding with him since July 1524. His treatise *Ob man langsam verfahren soll in Sachen, die Gottes Willen sind* ("Whether One Should Proceed Slowly in Things That Are God's Will") was greeted very joyfully by Grebel and his friends who, in October 1524, distributed booklets and writings by Carlstadt.[77] Later this connection also ceased.

In the meantime the movement in Zurich was spreading fast. An ever-increasing number of parents refused to have their children baptized. The Council threatened the recalcitrant parents with severe punishment. The parents based their stand on the Bible. Grebel reports this in a letter to his brother-in-law Vadian in St. Gall, dated December 15, 1524, and says, "I don't believe that persecution can be avoided. May God give us grace!"[78] At the end of 1524 Zwingli wrote his treatise *Gegen die, welche Ursache geben zu Aufruhr und wer die wahren Aufrührer sind* ("Against Those Who Cause Rebellion, and Who the True Rebels Are").[79] They were, of course, his former friends, Grebel, Manz, and the rest. Thereupon Grebel appealed to the Council in January 1525 and declared that he had

---

73 Zwingli, "Eine Christliche Anleitung an die Seelsorger," 17 November 1523, in *Ulrich Zwingli, eine Auswahl aus seinen Schriften*, ed. by G. Finsler *et al.* (Zurich, 1918), 379-93. See also Köhler, *Reformation H. Zwinglis*, 114; Nitsche, 14.

74 See *ME*, II, 771.

75 Muralt and Schmid, No. 13, pp. 11f.

76 *Ibid.*, No. 14, pp. 13-21; *Spiritual and Anabaptist Writers*, ed. G. H. Williams and A. M. Mergal (Philadelphia, 1957), 71-85; Bender, 282-87. About Müntzer see Bender, 116-20; Muralt, 19f.; Kautsky 150-52; Williams, 97ff.

77 See *ME*, I, 519-21. Bender, 108-10, 123; Muralt, 18f.

78 Muralt and Schmid, No. 18, pp. 29-31; Bender, 131; Kautsky, 156f.

79 Finsler, *Zwingli*, 441-66. See also Bender, 130, and article on Zwingli, section "Zwingli and the Anabaptists" in *ME*, IV, 1053.

never taken part in or provoked rebellion. He said anyone who had ever listened to him could witness to this, and he asked the Council not to stain its hands with innocent blood. Thereupon the Council fixed January 17, 1525, as the date for a public debate on infant baptism. The result of this debate was that Zwingli stuck to his opinion and Grebel and his friends stuck to theirs. The Council declared itself for Zwingli, just as Zwingli had come out on their side. Then the Council decreed infant baptism as a state law on January 18. Any person who violated the law was threatened with instant banishment from the lands of the state.[80]

In the meantime Jörg Blaurock[81] had joined Grebel's and Manz's circle. Blaurock had been a monk in the monastery of St. Lucius near Chur in the Grisons. He was born in Bonaduz on the upper Rhine, and his schooling was at Chur. Documents show that he was in Zurich in 1525. Apparently he had previously fought for the brotherly principles and ideas. We can see this in the tremendous energy with which he carried through baptism of faith in Zurich. It is noteworthy that the bookdealer Andreas auf der Stülzen (Andreas on Crutches), as well as Johannes Brötli, and Wolfgang Schorant (Uolimann),[82] who later led the Baptizer movement in St. Gall, also came from Chur. The latter had been a fellow monk of Blaurock's. When Blaurock came to Zurich in 1525 he was already married, which would have been impossible if he had still been a monk. He apparently was about thirty years old. He is described as a tall, powerful man, so that people would call out, "Here comes Strong Jörg!" He had fiery eyes and black hair, but was slightly bald-headed. He himself used his family name, "Jörg of the House of Jacob."

The Hutterian histories go on to say:

> He was told that there were other men there who were more zealous than Zwingli. He inquired about them and he came to them, namely to Conrad Grebel and Felix Manz, and talked with them about matters of faith. They united in this matter and in pure fear of God they confessed and felt it right that from God's Word and its preaching one should acquire a true faith active in love, and upon recognized and confessed faith and with a good conscience receive true Christian baptism in communication with God, to serve God henceforth in the divine blessedness of a holy, Christian life and to remain steadfast to the end even in affliction.[83]

Blaurock, the onetime monk, was the real man of the people among the early spokesmen. Nothing of the erudition of a Grebel, a Manz, or a Hubmaier! He was rather a man of the people who brought the movement to many, many people. Again and again we read in accounts of his life, "Suddenly one saw a crowd of people; in market places and in

80 Bender, 136; Williams, 120f.; Muralt and Schmid, "Mandate of the Council," No. 25, p. 35.

81 See *ME*, I, 354-59; also J. Loserth, *Georg Blaurock und die Anfänge des Anabaptismus in Graubündten und Tirol* (Berlin, 1899).

82 See articles on Brötli, *ME*, I, 439; Uolimann, *ME*, IV, 787f.

83 *Geschicht-Buch der Hutterischen Brüder*, ed. R. Wolkan (Vienna, 1923), 34-35.

squares they stood and listened to Blaurock talking of a better life, of conversion, of brotherly justice, and of God's Kingdom."

Blaurock, in his captivating eloquence, his popular appeal, was a man of dauntless courage. As a true apostle of Jesus Christ he went from house to house, from village to village, to establish the community of love in every place. We must tell more about him. First it is to be noted that he began baptism among the Brothers, shortly after the disputation of January 17 and the decree of January 18, 1525, when infant baptism was established under penalty of banishment in the event of violation. Blaurock asked Grebel[84] to baptize him on his faith. This took place, Jörg Blaurock then baptized the other fifteen Brothers and they straightaway held the Lord's Supper. Fourteen Brothers were arrested, and most of them were ordered out of the city immediately.

This first meeting of the newly emerging movement was gripped by deeply religious feeling. The Hutterian histories say of this meeting:

> It happened that they were together until fear struck them and came upon them, and they were compelled in their hearts. Then they began to bend their knees before the highest God in Heaven and called upon him as one who knows men's hearts, and asked him to grant that they might do his divine will and to show them mercy; for it was not flesh and blood or human wisdom that urged them, since they knew well what they would have to suffer and endure for it.
>
> After the prayer Georg of the House of Jacob stood up and asked Conrad Grebel for the sake of God to baptize him with the true Christian baptism on his faith and confession. And as he knelt down with this request and desire, Conrad baptized him, because at that time there was no Servant ordained to do such work. When this had taken place the others likewise requested of Georg that he baptize them; which he then did as they requested. And thus they together surrendered themselves to the name of the Lord in great fear of God, each one confirming the other in the service of the Gospel, and commencing to teach and to keep the faith. Through this the separation from the world and its evil works began.[85]

Zwingli once said of Grebel, "He talks as though the Messiah were here."[86] In this sentence two things are being said. One is that Jesus is the Messiah, that he will begin an earthly Kingdom of God in righteousness, and justice, peace, and brotherhood. The other is that this Messiah-King is present now in the true church. Zwingli could not tolerate this; for it meant that the church lives messianically, and Zwingli adds, "I did not understand in what sense he meant this."

This I would wish: that we live in such a way that Christ is the Messiah-King, that he is here, that we live in a messianic time because the Messiah-Christ is here! We don't need to make anything new, but to take up what is there and begin anew.

---

84 Bender, 137.

85 *Geschicht-Buch der Hutterischen Brüder,* 35.

86 Bender, 157; Egli, *Die Züricher Wiedertäufer,* 31.

OTHER BOOKS

by THE PLOUGH PUBLISHING HOUSE

The Early Christians: After the Death of the Apostles, by Eberhard Arnold. An unusual collection of early Christian sources covering the period A. D. 70-180. This book contains many texts so far inaccessible to the general reader, and gives comprehensive and challenging insight into the life and faith of the early Christians in a hostile, pagan environment.

Confession of Faith, by Peter Rideman. This book expresses the fundament of faith that has governed the life of the Brothers, known as Hutterians—originally an important part of the peace-seeking Anabaptist Movement of the sixteenth century—over the course of four centuries. As a historical record of the communal life of the Hutterians and their impact upon the religious, social and international life of that time, it is indispensable to all who wish for a full understanding of the Reformation and post-Reformation periods. This Confession was written by Peter Rideman in prison in 1545.

Christoph Blumhardt and His Message, by R. Lejeune. The first English translation. Tells of Blumhardt's life and gives nineteen sermons selected from the hundreds given by Blumhardt in his lifetime from 1842 to 1919 in Möttlingen and Bad Boll, Germany. Though virtually unknown to the English reading public, Christoph Blumhardt was one through whom many experienced the totally fresh and unconventional nature of Jesus' spirit.

Inner Words For Every Day of the Year, by Emmy Arnold, brings you a quote a day for a year, from the writings of men such as the Blumhardts, Eberhard Arnold, Dietrich Bonhöffer and others, who tried to put into daily practice their deepest faith regardless of the consequences.

Love and Marriage in the Spirit is a collection of talks and writings by Eberhard Arnold, selected from the times when he spoke at the weddings of the little community in Germany, or from the writings in which he addressed himself to what he considered one of the main life problems of young people. For Eberhard Arnold, weddings were a living opportunity to witness to the uniting power of God's love.